The ABC's of the Sacraments

. . . for children

Written by Francine M. O'Connor
Illustrated by Larry Nolte
Catechetical Advisors:
The Redemptorists

One Liguori Drive
Liguori, Missouri 63057-9999
(314) 464-2500

Note to Adults

The sacraments are presented here as love-encounters with God. For this reason, no attempt has been made to "teach" the sacraments or to prepare the young reader to receive them. Very simply, this book celebrates God's loving and saving presence in the child's life and in the lives of others. God's love is continuously expressed through the seven stepping-stones to salvation — the sacraments.

F.M.O.

Imprimi Potest:
William A. Nugent, C.SS.R.
Provincial, St. Louis Province
The Redemptorists

Imprimatur:
Monsignor Maurice F. Byrne
Vice Chancellor, Archdiocese of St. Louis

ISBN 0-89243-298-5

Table of Contents

A Big Day for Jesus

(Baptism)

Looking for Jesus,
looking all around,
down by the river Jordan one day,
there was a man called John
with a beard so long,
who baptized many who came his way.

John had a message straight from God,
"Get ready for a visit from the *special One*.
Change your ways, make good your days,
for the time is right for him to come."

THEN JESUS CAME WALKING.

"There," cried John,
"He is coming now,
the One who will wash
away your sin."
And Jesus spoke
to the man called John,
"Baptize me, John,
before I begin."

Then Jesus went down
to the riverbank,
down into the water
with the man called John.
And suddenly a dove
appeared from above,
and God's voice said,
"THIS IS MY BELOVED SON!"

So now the people knew
John's words were all true,
and the Baptizer's work for God was done.
Here now was the One
God said was to come,
and a new kind of baptism came with God's Son.

It happened long ago.
It happens still today,
Jesus comes from God to wash your sins away.
He gives you a place
in his own family,
and becomes your Brother on your baptism day.

Welcome to God's Family

(Baptism)

Hooray, hooray,
it's a wonderful day
for St. Monica's Parish,
you see.
We are coming together
to celebrate
a brand-new member
of our Church family.

For this is Amanda Jean's
baptism day,
and Amanda's family
is very proud.
We are all very glad
to be here today
to welcome our new
baby sister in God.

First Father Joe says a special prayer
for all who gather in the name of our King.
He reads from God's Word of the brand-new life
that this most holy sacrament will bring.

Then Father Joe traces the sign of the cross
with special oil on the baby's brow.
And her loved ones make this promise to God,
"We will raise this baby as your child now."

As the blessed water is poured on her head,
Amanda receives God's own life from above.
She's a brand-new child now, sinless and pure,
touched by the miracle of God's saving love.

Amanda wears a garment that is white
as a sign that her soul is white as snow.
And a candle is lit from the Easter flame,
the light of Jesus that will help her to grow.

Now God the Father of our Lord Jesus Christ
has welcomed Amanda in a very special way.
Praise Father and Son and Holy Spirit, too,
for the baby who joined our Church family today.

The Last Supper of Jesus

(The Holy Eucharist)

Jesus gave a supper.
All his friends were there.
Peter, James, and John
were by his side.
"I want to share
this meal today
before I go away,"
said Jesus on the night
before he died.

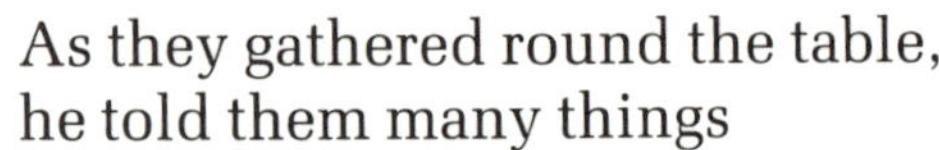

As they gathered round the table,
he told them many things

about a special sort of love that never ends,
like a mother loves her baby,
like you love your best pal —
that's the special love Jesus feels for all his friends.

He broke and shared the bread,
"This is my body," Jesus said.
"It will be given up so all of you may live."
Then he filled a cup and said,
"This is the blood that I will shed.
One's life is the greatest gift a friend can give."

This made his friends feel sad,
but he told them to be glad
because God the Father planned it all this way
so that Jesus could come again
and they would all know then
that the Son of God is in this world to stay.

We call it the Last Supper,
but that's not exactly true,
because he does it all again
for us at Mass.
And you can be right there
when Jesus comes to share
the supper that his people
call his last.

A Beginning that Never Ends

(The Holy Eucharist)

The first time I met
my friend Jamie
we spoke of many things
that we like.
Then I taught Jamie
how to play jacks
and Jamie taught me
to ride a bike.

That first time was just the BEGINNING
of a friendship getting better every day.
Jamie and I are such very good friends
we always have a good time when we play.

The first time I ever read a book,
it seemed such a hard thing to do.
Every new page was a mystery to be solved,
each word, a struggle to get through.

That first time was just the BEGINNING
of many happy hours of reading for me.
I never feel lonely if I have a book
to make me laugh or cry or keep me company.

The first time that I received Jesus,
it was a mystery I didn't understand.
It was exciting and new,
a bit scary too,
to hold the Lord Jesus right in my hand.

My First Communion day was the BEGINNING
of a love that will be in my heart to stay.
Jesus is as close to me as my own soul
and I can talk to him whenever I pray.

Once Jesus said, "Who eats this bread
will live forever and never die."
The promise of heaven began that day,
and that's a promise God will not deny.

Though all my BEGINNINGS were wonderful,
like learning to read or meeting a friend,
when I received Jesus the very first time
it was a BEGINNING that will never ever end.

The Disciples Get the Power

(Confirmation)

On the Feast of Pentecost, many years ago,
Jesus' friends were together in an upstairs room.
They spoke about the promise that Jesus had made
to send God's Holy Spirit to them soon.

Suddenly a sound like a strong, driving wind
shook the very walls of the house where they stayed.
Tongues of fire danced all around the room
and finally came to rest over each disciple's head.

The power of the Spirit in the wind and the fire
filled God's chosen ones with wisdom and grace.

They spoke of the Lord, their hearts burning with love,
to the crowd that had gathered in that place.

The power of the Spirit changed these simple people
into brave and fearless preachers of God's Word.
They traveled around to the villages and towns
to teach the world about Jesus, the Lord.

You, too, received the Spirit straight from God
on the day you were baptized in the Lord.
Like Christ's friends at Pentecost, you will be changed
by the power of the Spirit and God's holy Word.

Then will come a time, your night of wind and fire,
when you'll confirm your love
for Jesus from the start.
On your Confirmation day,
special power will be yours,
and God's Spirit will then burn in your heart.

Your Friend, the Holy Spirit

(Confirmation)

Who can take a frown
and turn it upside down?
Who can make a wrong
into a right?
Who can make your
heart pray,
brighten up a sad day,
and comfort you all
through the night?

Who can keep you strong
when you feel like doing wrong?
Who can teach you how you should behave?
Who understands your tears
and your secret little fears?
Who can even make a scaredy-cat feel brave?

Who did Jesus send
to always be your friend,
to keep the promise made before he died,
that after he was gone
you'd never be alone —
because someone would take his place
as friend and guide?

Who will come to stay
in a special sort of way
when you stand before the bishop
  on Confirmation day?
Soldier of the Lord then,
keeper of the Word then,
who will help you live the Christian way?

If you can't figure out
who this riddle is about,
it's about the One who makes you a better you.
This One shares the Lord's divinity,
third person of the Trinity,
God's own Holy Spirit . . . *that's* WHO!

A Jesus Love Story

(Reconciliation/Penance)

"Does God still love me?" you may want to know
if you commit sins or do something that's bad.
Well, Jesus told a story of the Father's love,
and it's the greatest love story we've ever had.

It's the tale of a farmer who had two sons,
but the younger one hated living on the farm.
"Give me all my money," he said to his dad
"and I'll leave this boring place and travel on."

So the younger son left, and he had a happy time
spending all his money on his newfound friends.
When his money ran out, so did his new pals
and the son was left with nothing in the end.

He begged for his food in the streets of town
and he slept beneath the cold night sky.
He longed for the comfort of his bed at home
and for the family that money could never buy.

He went back to the farm to beg and plead,
"Please forgive me, Dad, I want to come home."
The father had a party to celebrate the day
so he could welcome back the son who was gone.

You have a caring God whose love never ends.
It really doesn't matter how bad you've been.
Like the farmer's son, you can always "come home,"
God is your loving Father who'll always let you in.

That's how it happens in this sacrament of love.
You confess the sin and sorrow in your heart.
God is waiting to forgive you, his favorite child!
And from his loving grace he
will never let you part.

A Gift of Gladness

(Reconciliation/Penance)

Do you recall when you were bad
and Mom or Dad was feeling mad,
and then you said "I'm sorry,"
and everyone felt glad?

It's this special kind of gladness
Jesus gives each time you say
those magic words, "I'm sorry,"
that will wash your sins away.

Yes, Jesus has this gift for you,
something only he can give,
a gift to bring you happiness
as long as you shall live.

He gave it to his apostles
just before he went away,
and they have passed it on to you
in a very special way.

"Peace is the farewell gift I give,"
he told his friends that day.
"When you forgive a person's sins,
I will take those sins away."

What a super gift it is,
this gladness Jesus gives away,
your sins forgiven and forgotten,
and friendship that is here to stay.

A sacrament with a big, long name
will make this all come true.
REC-ON-CIL-I-A-TION
is God's gladness gift for you.

The Jesus Touch

(Anointing of the Sick)

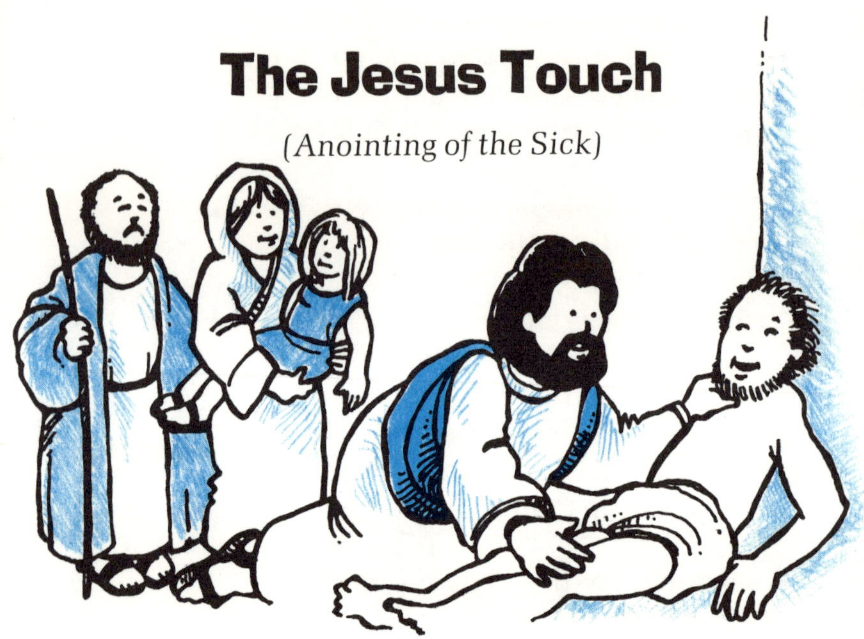

A long time ago in a faraway place,
the people all knew Jesus cared so much.
They'd bring their sickness and pain to him
and he would heal them with his touch.

Lame men walked and blind people saw,
when they felt the healing touch of our Lord.
And sometimes he'd heal them from far away
with just a prayer and a comforting word.

And still today, after hundreds of years,
Jesus has not lost his healing touch.
We call on his name and he is there,
easing our pain and comforting us.

He gave us the Anointing of the Sick,
so he could heal us from heaven above.
He's at our side when suffering comes
and he holds us in his arms of love.

Sometimes Jesus does take our sickness away,
while other times he helps us endure.
And sometimes he prepares us for heaven,
where sickness and pain are no more.

God shares the love of Jesus
with all suffering people on earth.
What a wonderful thing to have such a God
caring for us from our moment of birth.

Jenny's Grandma

(Anointing of the Sick)

Young Father Ryan came to the house
when Jenny's grandma was ill.
"Will you make her better?" Jenny asked.
He answered, "In God's way, I will."

First Father spoke to Grandma alone,
then the whole family circled her bed.
While they prayed together in candlelight,
Father anointed her hands and her head.

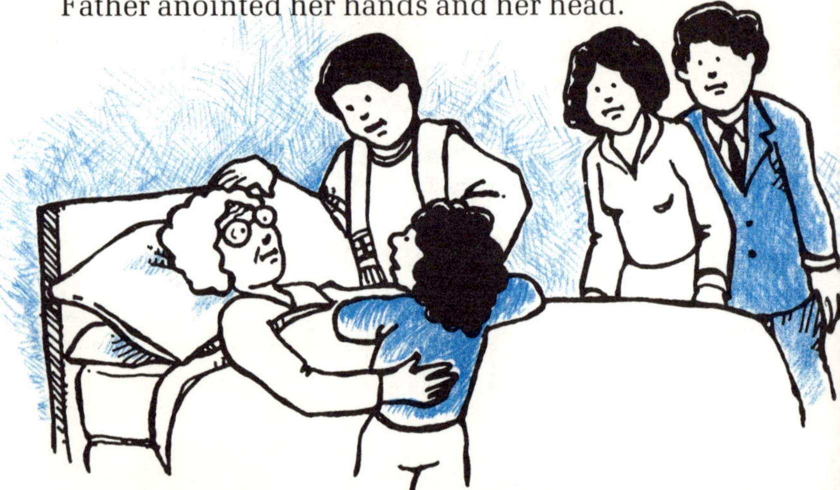

"This is so beautiful," Jenny said,
"the candles, the family, the prayers."
And Grandma agreed with a gentle smile,
"Our God is a God who cares."

"I've never been happier," Grandma said,
"and I feel all brand-new inside."
Then, with a beautiful smile on her face,
Jenny's grandmother died.

Jenny looked up with tears in her eyes.
"You said she'd be better!" the girl cried.
And she turned her back and walked away
from the priest who had told her a lie.

Father Ryan came to find her
and he took her upon his knee.
"Jenny, what I said is true,
in God's way, she's better, you see."

Then he told her about three happy things
on that special sacrament day:
"Grandma is happy, and
Grandma's with God,
and you'll meet her
in heaven someday."

Then Jenny remembered
Grandma's smile
and she smiled again
through her tears.
Father and Grandma had
told her the truth,
"Our God is a God
who cares!"

A Wedding Miracle

(Matrimony)

It was a wonderful day for a wedding,
and the bride was so lovely to see.
The best man came and brought the ring,
and the groom was nervous as can be.

Mary and Jesus were there on that day,
and the celebration was going just fine
until one of the waiters came to Mary
and whispered, "We've run out of wine!"

"They have no wine," Mary told Jesus.
(She was sure that he'd know what to do.)
"Please, don't worry," she told the waiter.
"Just do whatever Jesus tells you to."

Then Jesus said, "Fill six water jars,"
and the waiters obeyed with great haste.

"Now draw out some
water," Jesus said,
"and take it to the
headwaiter to taste."

The headwaiter sipped
the water slowly,
then drank as if
with great thirst.
He said, "Why, this is such a surprise.
This last wine is finer than the first!"

What a wonderful thing Jesus did that day,
turning water to wine for a bride and groom
so their wedding day would not be spoiled
by disappointment or sadness or gloom.

Now here's a surprise
for couples today;
they've an even finer
wine to share.
As they drink from the cup
at Communion time
the miracle of Jesus
blesses the pair.

Then Jesus remains in their life forever
to help them through worries and cares.
They are glad to share Jesus' special love,
and Jesus is glad to share theirs.

And Three to Get Married

(Matrimony)

It only takes two
to have a friendship,
and two can play catch
or run a race.
Two is enough to start
a special club
with a secret meeting place.

It takes just two to play checkers,
and just you and God can make a prayer.
You don't need a crowd to be happy,
just someone with whom you can share.

The sacrament of Matrimony starts with two,
one bride, one groom, very much in love.
But to stay in love their whole life through,
they need the special help of the Lord above.

They stand before the altar, hand-in-hand,
and promise to love eternally,
to make God a partner in all their plans,
so bride plus groom plus God become three.

Three to make the new marriage strong,
three to raise a loving family,
three to be together when things go wrong,
three for all the happy years to be.

Two is not enough for a Christian family,
the sacrament of Matrimony starts with three.

David Grows Up

(Holy Orders)

"What do you want to be when you grow up?"
Daddy asked David when he was four.
David thought for a long, long time,
until he couldn't think anymore.

"Maybe," he said, "just maybe,
I'll be like you, a super dad.
I'll hug all my children every day
and make them happy when they're sad."

"What do you want to be when you grow up?"
Mother asked David when he was nine.

David thought for
a long, long time,
but he couldn't
make up his mind.

"Maybe," he said,
"just maybe,
I'll be a policeman,
big and strong.
I'll tell the bad guys
how to be good,
and I'll help the people
when things go wrong."

"What do you want to be when you grow up?"
the teacher asked David in junior high.
David thought for a long, long time,
and then shook his head with a sigh.

"Maybe," he said, "just maybe,
I'll be a great teacher in school.
But I'll teach only happy things,
like 'God is love' and the Golden Rule."

When David grew up so handsome and tall,
God said, "David, come work for me."
And David said, when he heard God's call,
"A *priest* is what I *always* wanted to be!"

Then, in a sacrament called Holy Orders,
David promised Jesus, "I'll follow you."
Today FATHER David is a happy man,
doing the things he *always* wanted to do!

Listen . . .
It's Jesus Calling

Listen . . . do you hear a sound . . .
like snowflakes falling to the ground
or sunlight bursting through the trees?
Listen . . . it's Jesus calling,
"Come take my hand and walk with me."

He calls the tiny newborn babe,
"You're welcome to my family."

He calls his children to the Mass,
"Come and share this bread with me."

He calls you when your faith needs help,
"Let my Spirit lead the way."

He calls to you when you've been bad,
"I will wash your sins away."

He calls the dying and the sick,
"Bring all your sufferings to me."

He calls to every bride and groom,
"I bless your love eternally."

And some he summons with a special call,
"A priest forever you will be."

Jesus calls you many times
to come and meet him face-to-face,
through those sacred silent signs,
the seven sacraments of grace.

The feeling he gives is a wondrous thing
like the flutter of a butterfly's wing,
like popping buds on the maple tree,
like winter warming into spring.

Listen . . .
he is calling you,
"Come take my hand
and walk with me."

Also by Francine M. O'Connor

THE ABC's OF THE MASS . . . for children

This creative combination of verse and illustration moves step-by-step through the various parts of the Mass and includes simplified versions of many of the prayers that little ones hear every Sunday — but don't really understand. **$2.50**

THE ABC's OF THE ROSARY . . . for children

This little book does more than merely teach the formula and the prayers — it highlights each of the fifteen mysteries in a fascinating presentation that brings the story of Jesus to life. This book makes the rosary a prayer experience the whole family can share. **$2.50**

SPECIAL FRIENDS OF JESUS: New Testament Stories

This delightful book contains twelve lovable lessons and extra illustrations to make the book easier to read — and more entertaining — for younger children. "The Birth of Baby John," "The Little Man in the Tree," and the other wonderful stories in this 64-page book offer a special way to introduce little ones to some special people. **$3.95**

THE ABC's OF PRAYER . . . for children

This book helps children share their thoughts with God. Francine O'Conner and her daughter, Kathryn Boswell, put special prayers into delightful illustrated verses that make learning to pray fun. Verses like "My Morning Prayer," "Prayer Is Listening Too," and "Prayer for My Family" help children develop a good habit of praying daily. **$2.50**